CATHOLICS GOING GREEN

A Small-Group Guide for Learning and Living Environmental Justice

ave maria press AmP notre name, indiana

Founded in 1865, Ave Maria Press is a ministry of the Indiana Province of Holy Cross.

www.avemariapress.com

ISBN-10 1-59471-210-7   ISBN-13 978-1-59471-210-4

Cover image © Jupiter Images Unlimited.

Cover and text design by Andy Wagoner.

Living the Message features by Jerry Filteau.

Printed and bound in the United States of America.

CONTENTS

Preface   4

Using This Booklet   7

Session 1: We Walk on Holy Ground   11

Session 2: We Honor the Dignity   24
      of the Human Person

Session 3: We Stand in Solidarity   35

Session 4: We Share the Goods of the Earth   47

Session 5: We Champion the Cause   58
      of Global Human Development

Session 6: We Answer the Call to   71
      Conversion of Life

Resources   85

Additional Prayers and Psalms   88

PREFACE

Most of us spend our days pretty close to home. Even if we are away on trips, our thoughts are not far from those we love. No matter what our state in life might be, we want to be with our families, friends, and communities. This is a good thing. Closeness to family and friends makes our world go 'round. Without this closeness, love and fullness of life would elude us.

At the same time, our Catholic faith reminds us that we can't forget about others. Out of love, we're asked to look beyond our own fences at the larger world. For some of us, this looks like a rewarding adventure; for others, it's a bit frightening. Caring for brothers and sisters all across the world and taking responsibility for God's beautiful creation takes courage and generosity.

For many years, I was the director of the environmental justice program for the United States Conference of Catholic Bishops in Washington, DC. This organization had pastoral responsibility for many people. In my current work on behalf of the environment with an interfaith organization, I have another extraordinary opportunity to look beyond my own fences. Doing this work has opened my mind to some new challenges. More importantly, and has also deeply touched my heart. Working for environmental justice is, I believe, what God has called me to do.

Over the years, I have learned that Christ is present in the great work of caring for creation and the environment. After all, this beautiful planet that is our home is also God's gracious gift.

Caring for creation has deepened my relationship with God and others. In particular, it has called me to care more deeply about those living in poverty and on the margins. These are the people who suffer most because of environmental neglect and degradation.

Pope John Paul II said that "the aesthetic value of creation cannot be overlooked. Our very contact with nature has a deep restorative power" (World Day of Peace Message, 1990). I share this deep sentiment because I too have experienced nature in this way. It leads me to restoration and serenity. It also prompts me to contemplate God's beauty, wisdom, imagination, and love.

I have also seen the awful degradation that we humans have inflicted upon our planet. I believe that losing respect for God's creation diminishes not only people and animals, but also diminishes our relationship with our creator. John Paul's assertion that nature's beauty restores us is a very Catholic worldview and points us toward our responsibility as humans. We must care for God's creation and work to preserve its beauty. We need natural beauty to nourish and restore our spirits and we need Earth's goodness to sustain human life. We must become better stewards for our own sakes and for the protection of the most vulnerable members of the human family.

In our spiritual lives, we know that listening to the voice of God is not always easy. If we don't have time or don't take time to listen to the Spirit's prompting in our own hearts, we may find it impossible to "listen to nature." But that, as Pope Benedict XVI insists, is exactly what we need to do. Because he highlights environmental justice in many of his talks and public appearances, *Newsweek* has dubbed Benedict "the Green Pope." In a talk given in northern Italy during the summer of 2007, Pope Benedict told four hundred Italian priests, "We cannot simply do what we want with this Earth of ours, with what has been entrusted to us. . . . Our earth is talking to us and *we must listen to it* and decipher its message if we want to survive."

Each of the reflections in *Catholics Going Green* introduces a different aspect of our relationship with God, nature, and others. The themes treated here are drawn from the core principles of Catholic social teaching—particularly the 1991 United States bishops' statement, *Renewing the Earth*. As a whole, they ask us to reflect and talk about the natural environment and our responsibilities for it. The profiles that accompany these reflections show us how some Catholics are already taking up their role as stewards for the environment.

Once you complete this six-session program, you will have deeper reverence for creation. These reflections, quotes, prayers, stories, and conversation questions can spark your imagination and your commitment to "listen to the earth." Hopefully, you will be ready and willing to respond in your own way to the environmental needs around you. Our Church requires of us an ever-deepening relationship with God, with our precious earth, and with all our brothers and sisters, both within and beyond our personal fences.

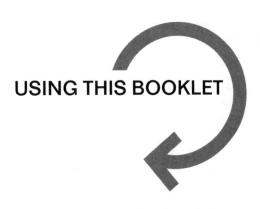

USING THIS BOOKLET

Y ou will likely be using this booklet with other Catholics who are as concerned about environmental justice as you are. It will be helpful to designate a group facilitator to help your sessions flow more smoothly. This can be one facilitator for all sessions, or a different facilitator for each.

The facilitator's task is neither highly demanding nor overly complex. It involves making sure that your meeting space is ready and that any needed session materials are available. For the most part, that means arranging for comfortable seating, bibles, a prayer candle, and perhaps recorded music or song sheets. Keep it simple. The facilitator(s) will need some skill at keeping the conversation focused and fair and at time management. Hints for facilitating follow on the next page.

The six sessions of *Catholics Going Green* invite you to: *read, reflect, discuss, pray,* and *take action.* Each session invites you to share the rich wisdom and social justice tradition of the Church. Learning about and discussing these teachings will help to deepen your relationship with our Creator, our Church, the Earth, and all its inhabitants. They will also help you see how environmental degradation brings the greatest suffering to the poorest people of our world. Hopefully, your conversations and reflection will inspire you to take action on behalf of protecting our Earth and our most vulnerable sisters and brothers.

The printed materials for each session provide a starting point for reflection, discussion, and action, but the real text of *Catholics Going Green* will be the shared stories, conversations, and changed behaviors of your small group. The heart of this program will be shaped by your group discussions, the actions you decide to take, and the subtle but important changes of heart, mind, and patterns of living that will come from this program.

May you come to learn and live more fully as *Catholics Going Green*!

Hints for Facilitators

If you've never had experience or training as a small group leader, ask for guidance from your pastoral leader or do a little online research about effective facilitating. Here are twelve hints to help you get started:

1. Be a good timekeeper. Start on time and finish on time—we suggest ninety-minute sessions. Your group should feel free to adapt the session length to meet their specific needs, but once you have agreed on a time-length, be sure to stick to it.

2. Make sure the room is comfortable, clean, and welcoming. Be sure there is a convenient place for refreshments if you plan on serving them. Ask for volunteers to take turns bringing snacks so you don't have to do it each time.

3. Be sure to have the following available for the closing prayer: a candle, bibles, and, if your group desires, appropriate music. Some sessions may require only one bible.

4. Allow about ten minutes at the end of each session for shifting into and completing the Closing Prayer. If you are not comfortable leading prayer, ask someone to fill this simple role. Either prepare the scripture reading for the closing prayer yourself, or ask another trusted group member to do so.

5. Encourage participants to read the preface and the section on using this booklet prior to the first session.

6. Each session follows the same simple format, using these six elements:

    ▸ Title and Thematic Quote

    ▸ Setting the Stage *A brief reflection from the author, Walter Grazer, that introduces the central themes and concepts for the session*

    ▸ Hearing the Church *One excerpt from a teaching document of the Church paired with a brief reading from a theologian, spiritual writer, or other relevant expert*

    ▸ Living the Message *A short profile of Catholics living out environmental justice, written by journalist Jerry Filteau*

    ▸ What Can We Do? *A list of possible action steps for groups, households, and individuals with space to write down action commitments*

    ▸ Closing Prayer

7. At your first gathering, take a few minutes at the beginning to let everyone get acquainted. Each person might introduce him- or herself and say very briefly what brings him or her to the group.

8. At the start of each subsequent session, have participants talk briefly about how they did on their action commitment(s) from the previous session. You may then want to use one of the prayers in the back of this booklet as a more formal beginning.

9. You will need to decide as a group if you will read through each session prior to or during your meetings. If you choose during, will you have one person read aloud, or each person read silently?

10. Use the questions throughout each session to facilitate conversation.

11. Keep in mind that you will likely have both introverts and extroverts in your group. The introverts will need to collect their thoughts, and perhaps listen to everyone else first, before they speak. By contrast, the extroverts will want to speak their way through what's on their minds. Be careful to create some silence for the introverts and to keep the extroverts from taking over the group. Introverts may need to be drawn out and extroverts gently reminded to give others the space they need to participate.

12. Remember that you, too, are a participant and be sure to share your own stories, insights, and questions with the group.

SESSION 1:
WE WALK ON HOLY GROUND

*God looked at everything he had made,
and he found it very good.*

—Genesis 1:31

Setting the Stage

How powerful this simple statement from Genesis is! So powerful that a fundamental teaching of our Catholic faith rests upon it. We believe that God is the creator. And, we believe, as the first book of the Bible tells us, that God found what he created to be very good!

In fact, you and I often share God's point of view. We find our world absolutely beautiful . . . and, of course, "very good." Have you ever looked up at the night sky and felt awed by its immensity and beauty? Or, have you watched, with childlike fascination, as a bee went about pollinating a flower? Or maybe you once climbed to a mountaintop. Exhilarated, you looked out in every direction to find a beautiful world spread out below. Many people call these unforgettable encounters with nature "God moments."

The Catholic Church takes this idea about the goodness of creation much further. The Church says that every part of creation is sacred or holy precisely because God has created it. In the sacramental worldview that forms the heart of Catholicism, creation is sign of God's presence and abiding love for us. As such, it is worthy of our profound care and requires our able stewardship.

Obviously, encountering God through nature is different than encountering God through the seven liturgical celebrations we call sacraments, or through the scriptures. Nevertheless, nature remains an important source of spiritual well-being in the life of the Church, and careful attention to our role as stewards of the Earth provides direction in the moral life of Catholics.

In the first Christian centuries, the sacramental vision of nature was much stronger than it is for many Christians today. Deeper Appreciation for nature was seen as learning about and drawing closer to God through the created order. Today, fueled by recognition of the current environmental crises, many Catholics are renewing this ancient vision. This renewal is evidenced in many places by the bold manner in which increasing numbers of Catholic parishes celebrate our sacramental and other liturgical rites. We see increasingly vibrant celebrations of baptism, confirmation, eucharist, rites of anointing of the sick, weddings, and funerals. All of these use things of the Earth such as water, bread, wine, oil, and fire—to point us toward God, present among us and loving us. We are a sacramental people, finding signs of God in all things—most fundamentally in the things of nature.

Recall an experience of nature that made you feel like you were on "holy ground." How was this a "God moment" for you?

Think of the sacramental elements of water, bread, wine, oil, and fire. Talk about what one or two of these say to you about God.

In modern times, the understanding that our earth is holy ground has faded for many of us. Our understanding that we should be gentle stewards of the earth has become distorted. There are many reasons for this shift. For one thing, we live very different lives today. Most of us are no longer so closely connected with the earth. Most people in developed nations are disconnected from agriculture and other work directly tied to the earth. School children too often are amazed to learn that their supermarket apples didn't come from the apple factory, but grow on trees!

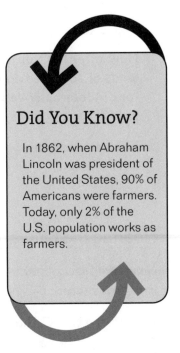

Did You Know?

In 1862, when Abraham Lincoln was president of the United States, 90% of Americans were farmers. Today, only 2% of the U.S. population works as farmers.

Because so many of us live and work in ways disconnected in conscious ways from the earth, we have a greater inclination to unknowingly or carelessly neglect or misuse this holy ground. Air pollution, global climate change, dirty and unsafe water, toxic waste, and many other environmental degradations confront us. In so very many ways, we are failing to be good stewards.

There are so many frightening signs that our earth is facing devastating problems. We can help by recapturing a deeper and closer connection with our earth and its needs, and by making some simple changes in the way we live that will allow us to become good stewards.

How often do you spend time outdoors, and in what kinds of activities do you engage? If you had more time for outdoor activities, would you take advantage of it? How?

In what ways are you already working to protect the environment?

Hearing the Church

Now, spend a few minutes reading and reflecting on what our Church has to tell us about the holy ground we have been given.

In 1991, the U.S. Catholic Bishops published a pastoral letter to American Catholics about environmental justice. The letter was called *Renewing the Earth: An Invitation to Reflection and Action on Environment in Light of Catholic Social Teaching*. The bishops explained that they were writing this letter because widespread destruction of the environment was increasingly obvious.

Did You Know?

70% of the world's marine species are at risk of extinction and freshwater animals are becoming extinct five times faster than land animals.

The whole universe is God's dwelling. Earth, a very small, uniquely blessed corner of that universe, gifted with unique natural blessings, is humanity's home, and humans are never so much at home as when God dwells with them. The Christian vision of a sacramental universe—a world that discloses the Creator's presence by visible and tangible signs—can contribute to making the earth a home for the human family once again. . . .

Reverence for the Creator present and active in nature, moreover, may serve as ground for environmental responsibility. For the very plants and animals, mountains and oceans, which in their loveliness and sublimity lift our minds to God by their fragility and perishing, likewise cry out, "We have not made ourselves." God brings them into being and sustains them in existence. It is to the Creator of the universe, then, that we are accountable for what we do or fail to do to preserve and care for the earth and all its creatures. For "the Lord's are the earth and its fullness; the world and those who dwell in it" (Ps 24:1).

Did You Know?

About 40% of all waste in the United States is paper, but nationwide we only recycle about 25–30% of our paper waste.

Renewing the Earth: An Invitation to Reflection and Action on Environment in Light of Catholic Social Teaching, III-A
U.S. Catholic Bishops Conference, 1991.

• • •

In fact, the beginning of our commitment to earth renewal is an encounter with Mystery through the uniqueness of the earth. If we are humble enough to allow the earth to be our teacher, we may find that through its many qualities and characteristics, God communicates with us. "Ever since God created the world his everlasting power and deity—however invisible—has been there for the mind to see in things he has made" (Rom 1:20).

The earth is not insensitive or devoid of communication; rather, the earth is precious, for it is the meeting place of God and people. Furthermore, the earth is open to promise, for it is fulfilled through our proper action and encounter. Insensitivities are not in the earth but in us. By sensing the earth we start to communicate. We receive an elemental word spoken here before us. Focusing on earth and not on distant heavenly bodies, our acts are rightfully close to home, but at the same time, we can begin our process by gazing out at the vista of heavenly bodies in order to realize our smallness and greatness—that paradox which our cradle and grave, the earth, shares.

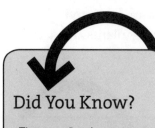

Did You Know?

The term "carbon neutral" refers to an energy source that releases no *additional* carbon into the atmosphere. That means that the released carbon doesn't exceed what was consumed by the energy source in the first place.

Renew the Face of the Earth
Albert Fritsch, S.J.
Loyola University Press, Chicago, 1987
p. 4.

Both of these brief readings call us to reverence the earth in order that it might help us know more about God, our creator, and about ourselves as a small part of God's creation. One way to reverence nature is to pray with it. How do you, or how can you incorporate nature into your prayer life?

What does it mean to look at our world as "holy ground"?

Living the Message

> *Dr. Russell Butkus is an associate professor of environmental ethics in the theology department at the University of Portland, a Catholic institution. He works with small groups that are concerned about the environment and wish to take on the big job of taking care of our "holy ground."*

When Dr. Butkus works with groups, he begins by having them check out their own local environmental issues at the U.S. Environmental Protection Agency's EnviroMapper website: www.epa.gov/compliance/whereyoulive/ejtool.html.

Visitors to the site can pull down a map of their ZIP Code area. Using tools on the map, they can identify polluted waters, sources of hazardous waste, local air quality, and other environmental concerns. "That's an eye-opener," especially in urban areas, he says.

Once there's been some discussion and reflection on what their own local environmental problems are, he asks people, "Why do we have these toxic waste sites? Why do we have these ambient air quality issues? What are we doing that's creating this? That's important because it gets into lifestyle issues. It raises the social/institutional causes that create environmental degradation." Once they have begun examining the relationship between lifestyle and environmental problems, Dr. Butkus helps groups see what they can do to work on problems in their own neighborhoods and towns.

Dr. Butkus then asks people to talk about what they are already doing to contribute to a solution—composting, recycling, turning down the thermostat on the hot-water heater, carpooling, using low-energy lighting, etc. "You affirm the activities that are currently going on, and people say, 'Geez, that's a great idea!'" He explains. "The bottom line is that if I'm more cognizant about my energy use, I'm not just probably producing less CO_2, but I'm probably saving some good bucks. And there's nothing wrong with that." People who are aware of their own household energy consumption are also more likely to pay attention to their neighborhood and community environmental concerns.

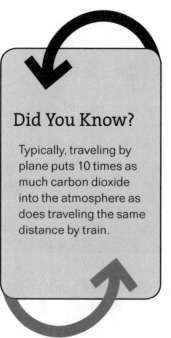

Did You Know?

Typically, traveling by plane puts 10 times as much carbon dioxide into the atmosphere as does traveling the same distance by train.

Butkus also discusses Church teaching and the theological reasons why Catholics are called to care for God's creation and the environment. The 1990 World Peace Day message of Pope John Paul II was on the environment. John Paul was the first pope to introduce "the ecological question" and connect it with Catholic social teaching. Papal statements since then, plus statements by the U.S. bishops, and pastoral letters by bishops individually or in regional groups have provided rich resources for Catholics to reflect on the environment and their responsibility to preserve and protect it.

Butkus says: "The reason we're doing this is that it goes back to Catholic mission and identity . . . the whole Catholic principle of sacramentality. Creation is a medium through which sacred reality is encountered. From the perspective of spirituality, it's developing the consciousness that God is revealed in creation."

Did You Know?

Americans spend about $11 billion a year on bottled water. It takes 1.5 million barrels of oil—enough to fuel 100,000 cars for a year—to make the plastic bottles to meet Americans' demand for bottled water, according to the Earth Policy Institute, a Washington, DC, environmental think tank. Only one in five of these bottles are recycled.

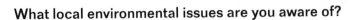

What local environmental issues are you aware of?

What specific concerns do you have about them?

What Can We Do?

No doubt you are learning more about environmental justice in our world. However, the environmental crisis is a huge and complicated issue. It's hard to know where you can help. Read through the following list of local activities and home-based projects that can help to restore the environment in small ways. Discuss these Action Options with your group as time allows. Then choose from the list or add your own ideas as Action Commitments for the week. Write your commitments in the spaces on page 22 and discuss your progress the next time your group meets.

Action Options

- Research environmental issues in your own ZIP Code area at the EnviroMapper website: www.epa.gov/compliance/whereyoulive/ejtool.html.

- Recycle at home and help organize efforts at work and school.

- Stop buying bottled water if possible. Use a reliable home filter if you are concerned about your local water supply. *Consumer Reports* magazine can help you find a quality product.

- Support local park and wildlife resources.

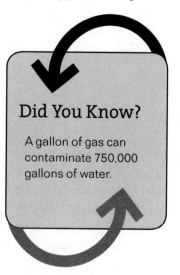

Did You Know?

A gallon of gas can contaminate 750,000 gallons of water.

- Take time out to sit in your backyard with friends and family. Appreciate the beauty of nature close to home!

- Learn more about your local watershed and ways you can protect it.

- Spread the word about the dangers of pouring antifreeze, oil, or other chemicals on the ground, into storm sewers, or down the drain. Take these toxic substances to your local waste disposal facility.

- Start using organic cleaning products such as lemon juice, baking soda, and vinegar. Or, use biodegradable cleaning products.

- Stop using chemical pesticides—try natural products instead.

- Let part of your landscaped gardening grow freely with wild flowers and other plants native to your zone.

- Consider planting local species of trees near your home, or donate and plant trees at your parish or another location in the community.

Write down your choices here:

Individual Action Commitment:

Group Action Commitment:

Closing Prayer →

Opening

All make the Sign of the Cross together

Scripture Reading

Reader: This reading is a wonderful expression of the sacramental or sacred nature of our earth.

Read Daniel 3:56–82

Blessing Prayers

Leader: In the Old Testament, "to bless" means to praise. It can also mean to wish or desire good fortune for a person, group, place, or endeavor. We now offer our own prayers of praise and blessing. (Leader should start with one or two brief prayers, then invite those of others.) For example: "God, I praise you for the lake where my family vacations each summer." Or, "O Lord, bless the children of our parish, and help them to find you in the beauty of creation."

Conclusion

You might wish to conclude your prayer by listening to an appropriate piece of music or by singing together. Or, simply close by praying the Lord's Prayer or one of the prayers at the back of this booklet.

SESSION 2: WE HONOR THE DIGNITY OF THE HUMAN PERSON

How beautiful are all his works!
even to the spark and fleeting vision!
The universe lives and abides forever;
to meet each need, each creature is
preserved.
All of them differ, one from another,
yet none of them he has made in vain,
For each in turn, as it comes, is good;
can one ever see enough of their
splendor?

—Sirach 42:23–25

Setting the Stage

As you already know, human beings are especially precious to the Creator. Genesis 2 reminds us, "God created man in his image; in the divine image he created him; male and female he created them." As Catholics, we acknowledge that human beings are at the pinnacle of God's glorious array of creatures. Human beings alone have immortal souls and are sons and daughters of God. And through the mystery of the Incarnation, Jesus Christ, the Son of God, became one of us, a human being.

However, we all learn about this innate dignity of human beings in different ways. I began to gain a deep respect for human dignity when I was a very young child. It began as I encountered the wonders of a flower garden!

An elderly neighbor tended his flower garden nearby with constant and loving care. Under his gentle guidance, I learned to name different flowers. I also learned to plant and water them. And then, in the silence of many summer afternoons, I slowly learned to appreciate the flower garden as God's handiwork.

Did You Know?

Nearly 1.1 billion people—roughly 20% of the world's population—lack access to safe drinking water.

I'm sure I was too young to consciously name this as a spiritual experience. But looking back, I can see that respect for all of God's creation was beginning in me. No doubt my parents also fostered that reverence for life. They were part of a larger Catholic community that holds a deep truth—respect for all life is tethered to respect for human life.

We can and should show deep respect for human beings in various life situations and at different stages of life. In particular, the Church calls on us to protect the most vulnerable among us—the unborn, the dying, the elderly, the stranger, the poor, the shunned or marginalized. This loving respect and care goes to the heart of who we are as followers of Christ.

When have you witnessed someone showing deep respect for a person overlooked or ignored by others? How did that affect you?

Witnessing such experiences can stir and shape us. And yet, while human beings reflect God most closely, the rest of

Did You Know?

11.7 million children in the United States live in households where people have to skip meals or eat less to make ends meet. That means that people are living with hunger or are at risk of hunger in one in every ten U.S. households.

creation desperately needs our respect and care as well. Other creatures reflect the Divine in simpler ways. Our Church recognizes this web of life. Caring for our neighbor in need fosters attitudes of respect for all of creation. And the reverse is true, as well. Coming to know nature —the gift of our Creator—should generate respect for our brothers and sisters everywhere.

The Old Testament reminds us that our human story has always been inextricably bound up with our fellow creatures—from the Garden of Eden on. In Eden, every hunger and every need of every creature had been answered. Adam and Eve's sin brought an end to that perfect harmony between all creatures. The Creator promised to send a Savior someday. When God later made a covenant with Noah after the flood, God made a promise to Noah, to Noah's descendants, and to "all mortal creatures that are on the earth." God promised that he would never again "send a flood to destroy all mortal beings." God set a rainbow in the cloudy sky as a perpetual sign of this covenant. Ever since, the rainbow has been a symbol of God's loving providence and care for creation.

Despite the many environmental problems in our world, do you see any rainbows—signs of hope? What are they?

Hearing the Church

→

Our Church has always shared the hope-filled truth of God's word. Now spend a few minutes reading and reflecting on what the Church tells us about cherishing and protecting both human beings and God's other creatures.

This is an excerpt from *The Ecological Crisis: A Common Responsibility*, the January 1, 1990, message of Pope John Paul II for the celebration of the World Day of Peace.

> The most profound and serious indication of the moral implications underlying the ecological problem is the lack of respect for life evident in many of the patterns of environmental pollution. . . . There are, however, certain underlying principles, which, while respecting the legitimate autonomy and the specific competence of those involved, can direct research towards adequate and lasting solutions. These principles are essential to the building of a peaceful society; no peaceful society can afford to neglect either respect for life or the fact that there is an integrity to creation.

• • •

St. Thomas Aquinas (1225–1274) was one of the greatest theologians of the Church. In his greatest work, The *Summa Theologica*, (Prima Pars, question 47, Art. 1), Aquinas discusses the divine imprint God has left on all creation.

> God produced many and diverse creatures, so that what was wanting to one in representation of the divine goodness might be supplied by

another . . . hence the whole universe together participates in the divine goodness more perfectly, and represents it better than any single creature whatever.

• • •

The following excerpt about St. Francis and his love of creation and all creatures is from *Care for Creation: Human Activity and the Environment* by Sr. Majorie Keenan, R.S.H.M. (Libreria Editrice Vaticana, Vatican City 2000, p. 37).

At times, Francis could perhaps seem to us to be too simple, too naïve, to content our complicated modern minds. We pass far too quickly over his suffering, his hard and penitential life, his long hours of contemplation, his courage in face of challenges of his time. What was the fruit of this life entirely given to God? A man that the animals considered their friend; a man who considered the sun and the moon as members of his family; a mendicant monk who gave all to the poor and who called death his sister. Francis dared to plumb the depths of the mystery of creation; *everything* was created for the glory of God; *everything* should render God this glory.

Which reading helps you see that respect for life and creation is the best starting point for our environmental response?

Living the Message

Carol Warren and Todd Garland of Webster Springs, West Virginia would enjoy the reading about St. Francis and his perspective on creation. Converts to Catholicism and lay associates of the Franciscan Sisters of Rochester, Minnesota, they have grown in their concern for the poor and the environment.

"I think the environment is the ultimate life issue," begins Carol Warren, former director of justice and life for the Diocese of Wheeling–Charleston in West Virginia. "If humans don't love and care for the planet the way God does," she explains, "eventually they will not only destroy the environment but themselves."

Carol and her husband, Deacon Todd Garland—who succeeded her in her former diocesan post—live out that commitment in their home on a hill near Webster Springs. Their small A-frame home gets most of its electricity from a set of solar panels and a thirty-six-foot-high wind turbine. Electricity from the commercial power grid comes into play only when the solar and wind sources are not enough. The solar panels are situated near their organic garden. They call the property the "Canticle of Creation," in honor of St. Francis.

For Carol and Todd, commitment to environmental care goes hand-in-hand with their passion for social justice and the sacredness of human life. In 1987, they left their jobs in Lexington, Kentucky, to go to Harlan County in eastern Kentucky. The couple were both raised as Episcopalians but became Catholic several years ago.

"We were drawn to the Church by its social teaching," Carol says. They were soon engaged in volunteer social outreach work in a couple of Lexington parishes. "We decided we liked that more than our jobs," she

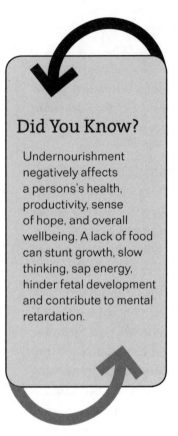

Did You Know?

Undernourishment negatively affects a persons's health, productivity, sense of hope, and overall wellbeing. A lack of food can stunt growth, slow thinking, sap energy, hinder fetal development and contribute to mental retardation.

recalls. Shelving their professional careers as well as their personal lives for a while, they decided to serve the Church and its people fulltime. They moved to the heart of Appalachia. "For a couple of years, we had no income at all," Carol recalls. "As we got more involved, we started picking up a little income. We were drawn there because we loved the people and the culture."

Then, in the mid-1990s, Carol and Todd encountered two Franciscan Sisters of Rochester, Minnesota. Carol says that connection came in Harlan County. The nuns had been sent by their order to minister in Appalachia. "They noticed we had Franciscan values and a Franciscan lifestyle, so they invited us to become associates," she explains.

When the couple moved to West Virginia, they bought a modest home with five acres on a hill called Potato Knob. They started investigating how to make their energy use more environmentally friendly. They settled on a combination of solar panels and a wind turbine as the most effective approach. The system cost $16,000, but the Franciscan Sisters helped them with a grant covering half the cost. "We never could have afforded it otherwise," Carol reports.

Carol says having solar and wind power for her home is also helpful when she speaks at hearings or other meetings on coal mining and the environment. On those occasions, when a representative of the mining industry reminds the group that they all rely on coal for their electrical needs, she says, "I can smile and say, 'No, I don't.'"

Does Carol and Todd's story help you see how you might serve the poor and the environment in your own way? How?

What Can We Do?

With your group, carefully consider and discuss the following Action Options. Some of these projects might help you put into action your respect for all life. Some are projects you will pursue personally. Others are more effective when they're done with your group.

Action Options

- Consider investing in companies that have "green policies," or go with "green investments."
- Organize a fundraiser for a local soup kitchen.
- Join or support your local chapter of the National Audubon Society or other non-profit environmental groups.
- Research companies and stores where you shop to see how they pay their employees, if they allow animal testing, and if they comply with environmental regulations.
- Volunteer at a local St. Vincent de Paul store or start a chapter in your parish to serve the poor.

- Use energy-efficient light bulbs. Add dimmer switches to prolong the life of incandescent bulbs. Lower or turn off lighting at night, inside and outside, to minimize the negative impact of artificial lighting on nocturnal animals.
- Purchase or make reusable shopping bags.
- Go paperless. Start receiving bills, newspapers, and magazines online.
- Look into programs that help you cancel all catalogues, credit card company offers, and junk mail.

Write down your choices here:

Individual Action Commitment:

Group Action Commitment:

Closing Prayer

Opening

All make the Sign of the Cross together

Scripture Reading

Ask several readers to take turns reading aloud Genesis 2:5–25, the second story of Creation.

Scripture Reflections

Share your own insights on this wonderful reading. What does this Genesis reading say about the relationship between human beings and the other creatures on our shared planet?

Conclusion

You might wish to conclude your prayer by listening to an appropriate piece of music. A psalm set to music would be especially appropriate since many psalms are prayers of praise to God for creation. Or, simply close by praying the Lord's Prayer or one of the prayers at the back of this booklet.

SESSION 3: WE STAND IN SOLIDARITY

For the first time since the beginning of human history, it is now possible—at least technically—to establish relationships between people who are separated by great distances and are unknown to each other

—Compendium of the Social Doctrine of the Church, #192

Setting the Stage

We all have moments when we want to pull the sheets up over our heads and hide from the world. Seemingly endless stories about wars, economic turmoil, and natural disasters are all pretty hard to take. The evening news is generally filled with such stories. Even closer to home, family problems, annoying neighbors, or simply the daily grind can send us running for cover—bed covers.

Sometimes, however, we feel uncomfortable or a little guilty that we're snug and safe when so many others are not. We wonder: "What can we do about the needs all around us?"

First of all, we must try to "tune in" to our brothers and sisters, far and near. The Psalms urge us to hear and respond to "the cry of the poor." If we can listen and learn, we can empathize with others. On CNN, we might "encounter" brothers and sisters living halfway around the world. Other people who need our attention, however, might be neighbors or fellow parishioners who are lonely, elderly, ill, or homebound.

In our hearts, we know that it is just and good to live a life that's connected with others—even people far away or people outside of our comfort zones. Recognizing the need for this connection and acting on it is what the Church means by *solidarity*.

Have you recently felt solidarity with people you don't know who were in pain or need? Were you able to help them? In what ways?

Don't feel bad if your answer was "No." We all have more to learn about seeing other people as God sees them. And we all need to grow in our commitment to the good of all people, a principle that our Church calls "the common good." In our "shrinking world," our need to care for each other is increasingly obvious. The global environmental crisis is heightening our awareness of that!

Did You Know?

One full standard toilet flush in the developed world uses as much water as the average person in the developing world uses in a day—for everything.

We live in a world with fewer real borders. Maybe you've met a foreign exchange student from the other side of the world. Perhaps you exchange e-mail with a soldier stationed far away. Maybe you've personally traveled extensively to far away places.

Today, the Church is asking us to recognize this growing interdependence, and the need to cooperate with other peoples of the planet. When it comes to environmental problems, everyone is affected and everyone is responsible.

In a sense, there's nothing new in this Catholic mandate to care for our brothers and sisters around the world. It builds on scripture. In fact, all of scripture pulls us closer to an understanding of God and his desire to see us care for each other.

In the Old Testament books of Leviticus and Exodus, God told the Jews to observe a "Sabbatical Year." Every seven years, the Jews were to let their lands, vineyards, and olive groves go untilled and un-harvested, allowing the poor to make use of them. Every fifty years, a Jubilee Year was observed. Land was returned to its original owners; prisoners were freed; debtors released from their debts.

The New Testament is also filled with stories of Jesus urging people to look beyond their own borders and boundaries. In the Parable of the Good Samaritan, Jesus tried to teach his followers that a "good neighbor" is anyone who cares for and unselfishly serves another human being.

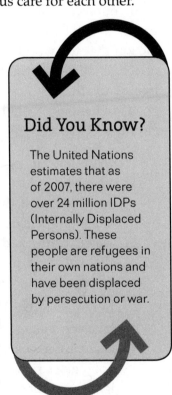

Did You Know?

The United Nations estimates that as of 2007, there were over 24 million IDPs (Internally Displaced Persons). These people are refugees in their own nations and have been displaced by persecution or war.

What scripture story or passage speaks to you about caring for others? Has it helped you to reconsider who your neighbor is?

Hearing the Church

→

Now read a little further to see what our Church has to say about reaching out to serve the world.

Two months before his death in June 1963, Blessed Pope John XXIII published his last encyclical, *Pacem in Terris* (Peace on Earth). In it, the dying eighty-one-year-old pope shared his conviction that the world would soon face challenges that could no longer be met by traditional political and social institutions. John wrote that the former Catholic teaching on the "common good" of nations would have to be expanded. Catholics would have to work for the common good of the entire human family.

> In the past rulers of States seem to have been able to make sufficient provision for the universal common good through the normal diplomatic channels, or by top-level meetings and discussions, treaties and agreements; by using, that is, the ways and means suggested by the natural law, the law of nations, or international law.
>
> In our own day, however, mutual relationships between States have undergone a far-reaching change. On the one hand, the universal common good gives rise to problems of the utmost gravity, complexity and urgency—especially as regards the preservation of the security and peace of the whole world. On the other hand, the rulers of individual nations, being all on an equal footing, largely fail in their efforts to achieve this, however much they multiply their meetings and their endeavors to discover more fitting instruments of justice. And this is no reflection

on their sincerity and enterprise. It is merely that their authority is not sufficiently influential.

Pacem in Terris, #133–134

• • •

The *Compendium of the Social Doctrine of the Church*, written by the Pontifical Council for Justice and Peace, is an overview of all of the Church's social teachings. It was published in 2005.

> The new relationships of interdependence between individuals and peoples, which are de facto forms of solidarity, have to be transformed into relationships tending towards genuine ethical-social solidarity. It is a virtue directed *par excellence* to the common good, and is found in a "commitment to the good of one's neighbor with the readiness, in the Gospel sense to 'lose oneself' for the sake of the other instead of exploiting him, and to 'serve him,' instead of oppressing him for one's own advantage."

Compendium of the Social Doctrine of the Church, #193

• • •

In 2001, twelve Catholic bishops of the Northwest United States published a joint letter titled *The Columbia River Watershed: Caring for Creation and the Common Good.* The bishops called on Catholics and others in the region to become better stewards of the Columbia River resource.

> We envision a place where all peoples are treated justly and authentic stewardship is the norm. . . . In that place, the place of our hopes and dreams, people will manifest a fidelity to their calling to

be images of God and caretakers of God's creation. There, people will recognize the inherent value of creation and the dignity of all living beings as creatures of God. There they will be ready to make sacrifices for the common good. In that place, the place of our hopes and dreams, there will be genuine respect for life, especially human life, and proper regard for the Creator.

Do any of these excerpts from Church voices inspire you? Can you foresee a place where "all peoples are treated justly and authentic stewardship is the norm"?

Living the Message

In the Diocese of Venice, Florida, the Church is trying to live as a "good steward" in the way it uses and shares a very precious resource—water.

Unlike the renowned canal city in Italy for which it is named, the diocese of Venice, Florida, faces serious water concerns. The Church in southwestern Florida is doing what it can to try to head off future water shortages for the entire region.

The increasing use of water is creating environmental problems throughout southern Florida, especially in the ecologically sensitive Everglades. The need for every individual and institution to be "good neighbors" in this crisis has become a significant social, economic, political—and religious—issue.

Neil Michaud, Director of the diocesan Peace and Social Justice Department, recalls that the Venice diocese began promoting awareness of local environmental issues in 2001. Educational events were often connected with Earth Day in the spring or near the feast of St. Francis of Assisi on October 4.

Then, in 2006, the Venice diocese helped develop an environmental statement signed by all of Florida's Catholic bishops. The statement, "Cultivating Care for All Creation," says that the growing ecological crisis calls all people to take more responsibility for the stewardship of God's creation.

"In southwest Florida, water is a crucial issue for both the civil and Catholic community," Michaud points out. The diocese, its parishes and other institutions have been giving much of their attention to water preservation.

At a diocesan-wide forum on water issues held at the cathedral in November 2008, leadership proudly showcased new landscaping at diocesan offices. This landscaping featured native Florida plants that thrive without regular watering or fertilizer treatments. The diocese hoped that this beautiful and environmentally friendly landscaping would serve as a model and an example.

Michael J. Holsinger, a horticultural scientist, sees landscaping as a significant environmental issue because in southwestern Florida "the landscape can use up to 50 percent of the water use of a household." Holsinger recently retired as Sarasota County Extension Director and is a member of the diocesan task force on environmentally sustainable architecture. The group advises parishes and other church institutions on environmental issues.

If Catholic institutions or individual Catholics replace their grass lawns—or even part of them—with native plants that don't require watering, they can reduce the local water consumption, Holsinger says.

Now, whenever parishes in the Venice diocese are faced with new building or renovation projects, they are expected to employ architectural, engineering and construction contractors who are familiar with environmentally sustainable building techniques and management.

Holsinger says it's extremely important for parishes and the diocese to do more than simply preach and teach about sustainable practices. They must also set an example by making their buildings and properties more environmentally friendly. If they don't, "how can you expect the parishioners to adopt sustainable practices in their homes and in their yards?" he asks.

How could your own parish or diocese take the lead in an environmental project for your larger community?

What Can We Do?

With your group, carefully consider and discuss the following Action Options. Some of these projects might help you work more effectively for the "common good." Some are projects you will pursue personally. Others are more effective when they're done with your group.

Action Options

- Investigate eco-friendly landscaping for your region through a local Extension office.

- Learn more about how climate change will affect those who are poor, especially in your region of the country.

- Individually, or with others in your group, volunteer at a homeless shelter or halfway house, reaching out as much as you can to your "neighbors."
- Learn more about adopting a simpler lifestyle that would mean reducing what you have and use.
- Use simple hand tools like rakes, clippers, and shovels, and reduce your use of electric or gasoline-powered tools.
- Buy the most energy-efficient household appliances you can afford.
- Use recycled paper and use both sides of paper sheets when possible.
- Buy products that have less packaging and that can be recycled.

Write down your choices here:

Individual Action Commitment:

Group Action Commitment:

Closing Prayer ──────────────────────────►

Opening

Consider opening prayer with an appropriate "musical statement" about our global family—brothers and sisters around the
world. One recommended selection is "We Are One Body" by
Dana Scallon.

Scripture Reading

Listen as a member of your group reads aloud the Parable of the
Good Samaritan, Luke 10:29–37.

Scripture Reflections

Briefly reflect upon and share ideas about what it means for
Christians to be good neighbors today. How can a sense of solidarity and understanding of the "common good" lead us to
good neighbor attitudes?

Conclusion

Together, pray this prayer from *Prayer for Peace with God the
Creator, Peace with All Creation*, Parish Committees and Prayer,
Parish Packet, United States Conference of Catholic Bishops,
1994.

Prayer

Lord, give us light and strength to know your will,
to make it our own, and to live it in our lives.

You desire justice for all;
enable us to uphold the rights of others;
do not allow us to be misled by ignorance
or corrupted by fear or favor.

Guide us by your wisdom, support us by your power,
for you are God, sharing the glory of Father and Son.

Help us to be good stewards of the treasures of your creation;
living persons, animals and fish and birds,
the lands and the seas.

We ask all of this in Jesus' name.
Amen.

SESSION 4: WE SHARE THE GOODS OF THE EARTH

If you wish to be perfect, go, sell your possessions, and give the money to the poor, and you will have treasure in heaven; then come, follow me.

—Matthew 19:21

As regards the ecological question, the social doctrine of the Church reminds us that the goods of the earth were created by God to be used wisely by all. They must be shared equitably, in accordance with justice and charity.

—Compendium of the Social Doctrine of the Church, #481

Setting the Stage

As everyone knows very well, the earth is fantastically rich in resources. Together, the air, water, fertile soils, numerous minerals, and the oceans can provide sustenance for the world's estimated 6.8 billion human beings, and for countless other creatures as well.

But there is a very frightening flip side to these blessings. If we ever have no clean air, no drinkable water, no healthy food, there will be no life! We should be grateful to God for the abundant resources that have made life possible and so remarkable up to now. Human intervention in nature, great imagination and wise use of technology have also helped many of us live our lives with wonderful benefits.

We need to remember that while modern science and technology can bring many benefits, they can also strain our relationship with nature. They can jeopardize, hurt, and kill people, particularly those who live at the margins of society. We are now more aware of how we can pollute the air, wash away irreplaceable soil, and waste water. The consequences of misuse, whether intended or not, are serious. Air pollution harms human health. Climate change makes droughts and floods worse. Damage to soil impairs agriculture. And wasting, hoarding, or contaminating water leads to conflict and disease. As Pope John Paul II put it, if we are not careful, and if we set ourselves up "in place of God" while we misuse nature, we can end up "provoking a rebellion on the part of nature" (*Centesimus Annus* 37).

Too often, a fundamental injustice is involved in the way we use resources. The benefits of a mining operation or an agricultural enterprise accrue disproportionately to the few, and not to the many. The "least" among us—those with few possessions—live on the margins of society and often at the edge of our consciousness. It is the poor who live on the flood plains or suffer the worst effects of the ravages of drought. They live in the substandard housing and eke out a living on marginal land and the slopes of mountains.

Did You Know?

Landfills in the United States are filling up and closing at the rate of approximately two a day.

When environmental conditions worsen, many poor people are forced to migrate. When storms come— whether they be natural disasters, war, or the storms of international market shifts—the poor are the first to be hurt. They lose their jobs, their homes, their health, and their hope. Modern environmental crises are intimately related to poverty. In 2005, Hurricane Katrina viciously struck our nation. It became a prime example of both the ravages of nature and of humankinds' failure to respond fairly and efficiently. It was the poor of New Orleans who suffered—and still suffer—the most.

In 2005, almost 1.4 billion of the world's population lived below the international poverty line, earning less than $1.25 per day.

How do you react when poor people are the primary victims of disasters or tragedies? Does it somehow seem "inevitable"?

Individually, it's hard to know what to do when earthquakes, typhoons, or hurricanes strike people who can least afford any kind of trouble. Of course, we can donate toward disaster relief funds. But it is largely the domain of governments, international organizations, and agencies to help.

On the other hand, governments, organizations, and agencies are made up of people—people with mindsets and values. As much as we can, we must help to shape governments and organizations. Those who speak in our name should act with our values.

One value, of course, is that nature's resources must be shared on a more equitable basis. Our Church uses the term "the universal destination of goods" in referring to the moral obligation to share with our brothers and sisters. The goods of the earth are not meant to be hoarded by or for a few select people. Our environmental problems today are global in scope. Responding to these problems will require cooperation, solidarity, and a just distribution of resources. This offers a path to provide dignity for the poor, and grace and redemption for all.

Earning a profit is a good thing, but the search for endless profits must never take precedence over the search for justice and a concern for our neighbor. Do you remember the Gospel story that Jesus told about the rich man who had the sick and ragged man, Lazarus, begging for help outside his door? The parable is found in Luke 16:19–31. Jesus makes it clear that the rich man, sometimes known as "Dives," was condemned because he heartlessly ignored Lazarus.

In your own community, are there needy people who are being overlooked or ignored? Who are they? Can you see a way to help them?

Hearing the Church

Now read what our Church says about sharing wealth and sacrificing self-interest for needy people who are too often ignored.

In this excerpt from Pope Benedict's 2007 New Year's Day address, the pope talks about competition between industrialized nations for resources and the disadvantaged position of poor countries:

> In recent years, new nations have entered enthusiastically into industrial production, thereby increasing energy needs. This has led to an unprecedented race for available resources.

Meanwhile, some parts of the planet remain backward and developmentally blocked, partly because of the rise in energy prices. What will happen to these peoples? What kind of development, or non-development, will be imposed on them by the scarcity of energy supplies? What injustices and conflicts will be provoked by the race for energy sources? And what will be the reaction of those excluded from this race? These questions show how respect for nature is closely linked to the need to establish, between individuals and between nations, relationships that are attentive to the dignity of the person and capable of satisfying his or her authentic needs.

Pope Benedict XVI
Message of His Holiness Pope Benedict XVI for the Celebration of the World Day of Peace: Human Person, the Heart of Peace
January 1, 2007, #9.

•   •   •

Dorothy Day (1897–1980) was a twentieth-century American Catholic who brought new awareness to the plight of the needy. With Peter Maurin, she founded the Catholic Worker movement to help and offer hospitality to the poor. Day encouraged people to follow the example of Matthew 25, performing the works of mercy every day. She adopted voluntary poverty and recommended it for others.

We need always to be thinking and writing about poverty, for if we are not among its victims its reality fades from us. We must talk about poverty, because people insulated by their own comfort lose sight of it. And maybe no one can be told;

maybe they will have to experience it. Or maybe it is a grace which they must pray for. We usually get what we pray for, and maybe we are afraid to pray for it. And yet I am convinced that it is the grace we most need in this age of crisis, this time when expenditures reach into the billions to defend "our American way of life." Maybe this defense itself will bring down upon us the poverty we are afraid to pray for.

The Catholic Worker
May 1952

Living the Message

Volunteers at the Catholic Charities Thrift Store in Panama City, Florida, may not have read what Dorothy Day said about staying in touch with the reality of poverty, but many would likely agree that the hard reality of poverty should always be in front of us so that the poor are not forgotten.

To share goods: quality used clothing, furniture, and housewares. That's the reason the Catholic Charities Thrift Store was opened years ago in Panama City, Florida. It is a logical outreach from the diocesan Catholic Charities office to needy people in this largely rural diocese, the diocese of Pensacola-Tallahassee in northwest Florida.

"I think that Catholic Charities has similar thrift stores in many dioceses," explains Mark Dufvo, Executive Director of Catholic Charities of Northwest Florida. Such stores are ideal for several reasons. They offer needy people goods at affordable prices, and they return the proceeds to subsidize other Catholic Charities ministries. Dufvo thinks the store in Panama City was founded back in the

1980s. His office is in Pensacola, but he follows what's happening at the Thrift Store, which is open four days a week from 9 a.m. to 2 p.m.

Did You Know?

Poor nutrition and calorie shortages result in death or disability for nearly one in three of the world's people, according to the World Health Organization.

Dufvo figures that the thrift store is a good and growing expression of the Catholic and Christian value to help those in need. It is conveniently located in Panama City in this diocese of eighteen largely rural counties. This diocese, he says, is "definitely mission territory." Only five percent of the diocesan population is Catholic.

Andrea "Andie" Casarez has been the thrift store's manager for about a year and has some pretty ambitious goals for its future. She's trying to boost her team of regular volunteers so that the store can open five days a week, Monday through Friday. "We have about twelve people on staff—Catholic and non-Catholic," Andie says. "Some of them are retired; some are women who don't work but like volunteering here." Volunteers sort and rack clothing, staff the cash registers, assist with furniture pickups, make signs, and cheerfully welcome customers, helping them to find what they need. Some volunteers maintain the store's attractive website at http://catholiccharitiesnwfl.org/17-Thrift-Store.

Being open every weekday during usual business hours will help raise the thrift store's profile in the community, Andie thinks. And because of the economic crisis, that's more important every day. It is definitely a service to the unemployed, people with very low incomes, and elderly people on fixed incomes. People in need still have their pride. They would like to be able to buy clothing or furniture at prices they can afford. The thrift store operation actually has two buildings—a retail facility "front store" and a warehouse where larger items such as furniture and appliances are dropped off and stored.

Andie is also working very hard to build relationships with local businesses in Panama City and beyond. She hopes to increase the number of retailers who donate salable items to the store, thereby helping to create a community-wide partnership of care and response. Encouraging people to give so that the store has plenty to offer to needy people—that's what it's all about.

> **Does your community have a thrift store like the one in Panama City? Have you ever shopped or offered to volunteer at such a store? Do you think that efforts like this really help to "share the wealth"?**

What Can We Do?

Now consider and discuss the following Action Options. Some of these projects might help you see new ways to share wealth and inspire others to do the same. Some are projects you will pursue personally. Others are more effective when they're done with your group.

Action Options

- Give up having your own garage sales and give "gently used" items to a St. Vincent de Paul or other thrift store where items are re-purposed to the advantage of many.

- Plan several low-cost menus for yourself or your family each week, and donate the difference in price to a local food pantry or soup kitchen.

- Consider organizing or supporting local community gardens to help supply fresh and nutritious vegetables for those who can't afford them.

- At your own home, collect rainwater to water houseplants.

- Run dishwashers and washing machines with full loads only.

- Buy CFL bulbs and install them throughout your house and place of business.

- Donate textiles (clothing, draperies, etc.) to St. Vincent de Paul, Goodwill, or Salvation Army thrift shops. These are used by many artisans to create new and useful products.

- Make lunches with reusable food and drink containers, avoiding disposable packaging and containers.

- Turn off lights and other electronic devices when not in use. Unplug as many electronics as possible when they are not in use. Turn off energy strips and surge protectors when not in use—especially overnight.

- Minimize your own food waste at home by incorporating leftovers into other meals or freezing them for another meal.

Write down your choices here:

Individual Action Commitment:

Group Action Commitment:

Closing Prayer

Opening

All pray the Our Father together

Scripture Reading

Reading from Matthew 25:31–46.
Listen to Matthew 25:31–46, a passage titled "The Judgment of the Nations." Then, as a group, reflect on what Jesus says we must do—feed the hungry, give drink to the thirsty, clothe the naked, etc.

Petitions.

Offer petitions to strengthen ministries that are already committed to the Matthew 25 mandate. Include your own individual prayers for the poor and needy of the world. For example: "God, please strengthen and bless the food pantry at St. Joseph's"; "God, please help me find a way to welcome strangers," etc.

Conclusion

You might wish to conclude your prayer by listening to or singing together an appropriate musical selection. Or, simply close by praying the Lord's Prayer or one of the prayers at the back of this booklet.

SESSION 5: WE CHAMPION THE CAUSE OF GLOBAL HUMAN DEVELOPMENT

The Lord God then took the man and settled him in the garden of Eden, to cultivate and care for it.

— Genesis 2:15

Stewardship implies that we must both care for creation according to standards that are not of our own making and at the same time be resourceful in finding ways to make the earth flourish.

—Renewing the Earth, III-A

Setting the Stage

What a beautiful garden God has fashioned for us on this planet! Every day is a miracle, and there is such an abundance of flowers, plants, and creatures on land, in the sea, and in the air that we have not even discovered or named. God made human beings stewards for the earth.

But what does this stewardship mean?

The usual meaning of stewardship involves taking responsibility for another person's property or financial affairs. Historically, stewardship was the responsibility given to household servants to bring food and drinks to a castle dining hall. Later, the term was expanded to describe the responsibility a household employee had for managing household or domestic affairs. That's the sort of steward Jesus described in the Parable of the Dishonest Steward in Luke 16:1–8. In this story, the steward apparently had full authority to handle the household for his rich employer. The angry master discovered that his steward had squandered his resources. For this reason—not for dishonesty—the steward was in big trouble and was about to be fired.

Today, Catholics are trying to understand what it really means to be environmental stewards. We don't have much control over what happens with rainforests in other countries, but there are plenty of ways to start closer to home. The steward's role begins with careful attention—a listening to what is happening around him or her, in nature, among his or her neighbors. And we must listen, of course, to God, the proprietor of our house. A steward does not have independent authority, but a borrowed authority. True authority belongs to the head of the house, the proprietor. Most of all, a steward must make sure that what he or she

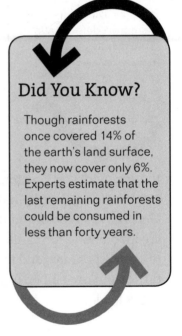

Did You Know?

Though rainforests once covered 14% of the earth's land surface, they now cover only 6%. Experts estimate that the last remaining rainforests could be consumed in less than forty years.

has responsibility for is well cared for and not neglected. The consequences of lazy or selfish stewardship are increasingly dangerous and deadly for the entire world.

For instance, the rainforests of the world, great treasuries of unique plant and animal species, are being cleared and destroyed. Most rainforests are being cleared for timber and then developed for farming or ranching operations by some of the world's largest corporations—Mitsubishi Corporation, Georgia

Did You Know?

Experts estimate that we are losing 137 plant, animal, and insect species every day due to rainforest deforestation. That equates to 50,000 species a year.

Pacific, Texaco, and Unocal. In the meantime, indigenous tribes are wiped out.

Not only is the loss of unique civilizations of tribal peoples a great tragedy, but the disappearance of untested plant species threatens world health. Hundreds of prescription drugs are derived from plants. In fact, some authorities estimate that one-fourth of all pharmaceutical products produced in western nations come from rainforest ingredients. Most of the disappearing tropical trees and plants have not been tested by scientists for their therapeutic potential.

The Church wants us to see that though God, our Creator, is the head of the house and the proprietor of creation, he has entrusted us with an awesome role. God wants his sons and daughters to be involved in protecting creation and assuring its welfare and bounty. It is the job given to our first parents and inherited by every generation. It is often difficult to remember, however, that the bounty of the earth belongs to all.

In what ways do you and your family, community, and nation benefit from the earth's bounty? Is equitably sharing the bounty of the earth a reasonable goal, or a foolish hope?

Authentic human development and good stewardship assume that we are growing in respect—for ourselves, our neighbors and the rest of creation. In "Renewing the Earth," their 1991 pastoral letter on the environment, the U.S. bishops explained that this equitable distribution and development of wealth means sharing not only the earth's natural physical resources, but also technological developments and scientific knowledge.

Did You Know?

Every year in developing countries, nearly 16 million children die from preventable and treatable causes.

The modern world has had many good reminders that resources must be distributed equitably.

On September 5, 1997, eighty-seven-year-old Mother Teresa of Calcutta died in India, her adopted homeland. Hindus, Muslims, Christians, and those with no specific religious faith all mourned her. More than any other single religious figure in modern times, Mother Teresa had reminded the wealthy and the comfortable that they must not forget or forsake the poor. Those with wealth and resources should give, not just out of their abundance, but until it hurts. That is the way Jesus gave and loved, she said.

Also in 1997, a PBS television documentary called *Affluenza* struck a chord with many Americans. "Affluenza," as the program explained, is an epidemic of over-consumption and materialism that afflicts many people in the developed nations of the world. Many viewers responded and began to consider the costs of this materialism in their own lives and in the lives of others. A sequel, *Escape from Affluenza*, aired a year later and was just as effective and popular. Many people rediscovered what they already knew: "keeping up with the Joneses" was pointless, empty, and wrong.

Hearing the Church

→

Moderation in all things and a genuine respect for nature and other creatures can help ensure that we will carefully tend the garden God has placed us in. Now spend some time reading and reflecting on what our Church is saying about God's call to stewardship.

Pope Benedict XVI has often said that the doctrine of creation has been neglected in modern theological reflection. Trying to address the environmental crisis without recognizing the "indissoluble bond" between creation and redemption will be fruitless. In particular, we need the Eucharist, the pope says, which unites us to God who is both Creator and Redeemer.

The world is not something indifferent, raw material to be utilized simply as we see fit. Rather, it is part of God's good plan, in which all of us are called to be sons and daughters in the one Son of God, Jesus Christ (cf. Ephesians 1:4–12). The justified concern about threats to the environment present in so many parts of the world is reinforced by Christian hope, which commits us to working responsibly for the protection of creation. The relationship between the Eucharist and the cosmos helps us to see the unity of God's plan and to grasp the profound relationship between creation and the

Did You Know?

People in developing countries are more than twenty times as likely to be affected by climate-related disasters than those in the developed world.

"new creation" inaugurated in the resurrection of Christ, the new Adam.

Sacramentum Caritatis (the Sacrament of Charity), 2007, #92.

• • •

Fr. John Chryssavgis, a priest of the Greek Orthodox Church, is a professor of theology at Holy Cross Greek Orthodox School of Theology in Brookline, Massachusetts, and the director of the Religious Studies program at Hellenic College, where he also established the Environment Office. The author of more than ten books, he currently serves as theological advisor to the Ecumenical Patriarch on environmental issues.

> The connection with land and animals is neither superficial or sentimental; it is deeply theological. It stems from the inner conviction of these hermits [the early monastics] that God created the world; and this implies that God loves and cares for the world, as well as for all that is in the world, both animate and inanimate. The desert elders were, in the most intense manner, "materialists." Everything—including simple matter—really mattered! In God's eyes, both animals and sand dunes are of importance and have their place; in Heaven, birds and trees are not excluded.

In the Heart of the Desert: The Spirituality of the Desert Fathers and Mothers
World Wisdom, Inc. 2003, p. 87

• • •

Mother Teresa of Calcutta, a native of what is now Macedonia, joined an Irish missionary order of sisters at the age of eighteen and was sent to India the following year. In 1948, she founded the Missionaries of Charity to serve "the poorest of the poor." In the 1970s and '80s, Mother Teresa and her work became internationally known as she promoted service to the needy in every nation.

> **The unwanted:** The biggest disease today is not leprosy or tuberculosis, but rather the feeling of being unwanted, uncared for and deserted by everybody. The greatest evil is the lack of love and charity, the terrible indifference towards one's neighbor who lives at the roadside assaulted by exploitation, corruption, poverty and disease.

Something Beautiful for God
Malcolm Muggeridge
Harper & Row Publishers, CA, 1973, p. 55.

What discipline or sacrifice would help you and your family to share your personal resources? What would "hurt" the most?

Living the Message

In recent years, many people from churches in Michigan's Upper Peninsula have sacrificed hours and hours of time collecting, sorting, and properly disposing of unused electronics, pharmaceuticals, and hazardous household wastes. "Earth Keepers," as the program is called, isn't really global in its focus, and it doesn't make boasts about "saving the planet." But this well-focused, annual Earth Day program invites ordinary people to become good stewards close to home.

On April 28, 2006, church parking lots across Michigan's Upper Peninsula overflowed with old computers and monitors, televisions, stereos, video recorders and players, cell phones, and other electronic waste. The three-hour Saturday morning Earth Day collection brought in some 320 tons of used electronic equipment at twenty-eight collection sites—more than two pounds for every man, woman, and child living on the peninsula, and triple what organizers had expected.

The previous April, the churches had collected more than forty-five tons of hazardous household products such as old oil paint, solvents, pesticides, batteries, and household cleaners.

In April 2007, they concentrated on unwanted pharmaceuticals sitting in medicine cabinets in people's homes. That year, the program collected more than two thousand pounds of outdated or unused prescription and over-the-counter drugs for proper disposal.

Did You Know?

Over 150 million mobile phones are purchased every year in the United States, and over 425,000 are thrown away every day.

The annual Earth Keepers environmental campaign involves people from nine different faiths—Catholic, Lutheran, Methodist, Presbyterian, Jewish, Buddhist, Unitarian, and Baha'i. Front and center, however, are Catholics from the Marquette diocese, which covers the entire peninsula.

Carl Lindquist, the group's director, says that Earth Keepers designates twenty or more collection sites in geographically strategic locations around the peninsula.

Participating churches in the area send volunteers to each location to help handle the incoming waste materials.

"It actually took us several weeks to get it all sorted and appropriately hauled away," he says. Various computer components and other electronic devices contain an array of toxic heavy metals, including mercury, cadmium, chromium, barium, and arsenic. Although the amount of toxic materials in a single unit is small, studies have shown that even minute amounts of these toxins pose a variety of environmental dangers. Some of these toxins may work their way up the food chain and pose serious health hazards to people, especially for unborn children, infants, and toddlers.

Lindquist is always happy to discuss the unique collaboration of Earth Keepers with the 150 individual congregations that participate in the collections. It's a natural fit, he says. "They had the enthusiasm and we had the logistical and technical expertise as well as some funding to help coordinate these things."

The diocesan bishop, Alexander Sample, also has plenty of praise for this annual interfaith stewardship effort. "I don't know of any faith tradition that teaches us it's okay to trash the creation that God has given us," Sample observes. This program helps to prevent toxic contamination. "It's one of those things that we can do together."

Have you worked with a group facing big jobs or major challenges? What shared values helped the group get the job done?

What Can We Do?

Continue to reflect on what Catholics in Michigan's Upper Peninsula are doing. Then consider and discuss the following Action Options. Some of these projects might help you and your group to develop new approaches to stewardship in your part of the world. Some are projects you will pursue personally. Others are more effective when done with your group.

Action Options

- Investigate programs that match needy "sister" parishes with more affluent parishes that can help them.

- Support Habitat for Humanity or similar programs that build and donate homes to those who can't afford them.

- Research and discuss "affluenza," the epidemic of over-consumption.

- Learn more about underdeveloped countries and their needs.

- Consider donating to international aid organizations like Catholic Relief Services, OxFam, or other groups that work to improve living conditions for those in underdeveloped countries.

- Plan regularly scheduled fundraisers at your parish to support organizations dedicated to human development.

- Buy organic and fair trade items (coffee, clothing, jewelry, etc.) that pay just prices to farmers and craftsmen in under-developed countries.

- Ask your local stores to stock organic and fair trade supplies.

- Organize a local event for Earth Day, World Water Day, World Bread Day, or World AIDS Day.

Write down your choices here:

Individual Action Commitment:

Group Action Commitment:

Closing Prayer

→

Opening

Listen to or sing together a song that celebrates the unity of the human family. Several to consider are "Gather Your People," by Bob Hurd or "In This Place," by Trevor Thomason and Victoria Thomson.

Scripture Reading

Listen as one member of your group reads Mark 8:1–10, The Feeding of the Four Thousand. Pause in silent reflection. Then share responses about the way Jesus fed hungry people and involved his disciples in the project. What messages can you find in this Gospel for modern followers of Jesus?

Petitions

Offer petitions for a new spirit of compassion toward those in poverty and for the underdeveloped areas of our nation and the world. Pray for a new approach to stewardship and responsibility for all of Creation. Use a petition response such as "Lord of Creation, hear our prayer."

Conclusion

Read together the following prayer from *Catholic Household Blessings and Prayers*

> All powerful God,
> we appeal to your tender care
> that even as you temper the winds and rains
> to nurture the fruits of the earth
> You will also send upon them the gentle shower
>   of your blessings.
> Fill the hearts of your people with gratitude,

that from the earth's fertility
the hungry may be filled with good things
and the poor and needy proclaim the glory of
   your name.
We ask this though Christ the Lord.
Amen.

"Assumption Day Blessing of Produce" in
   Catholic Household Blessings and Prayers
   United States Conference of Catholic
   Bishops, 1988, p. 172.

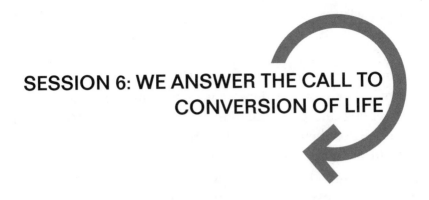

SESSION 6: WE ANSWER THE CALL TO CONVERSION OF LIFE

*Go into the whole world and proclaim
the gospel to every creature.*

—Mark 16:15

*The environmental crisis of our own
day constitutes an exceptional call
to conversion. As individuals, as
institutions, as a people, we need a
change of heart to save the planet
for our children and generations yet
unborn. . . . Only when believers look to
values of the Scriptures, honestly admit
their limitations and failings, and commit
their selves to common action on behalf
of the land and the wretched of the
earth will we be ready to participate
fully in resolving this crisis.*

**Renewing the Earth: An Invitation
to Reflection and Action on Environment
in Light of Catholic Social Teaching, #V-C.
U.S. Catholic Bishops Conference, 1991.**

Setting the Stage

Most of us probably don't think of tending to God's garden
and caring for creation as evangelization, that is, spreading the
Good News about God's love and the salvation he offers. But

this present historical moment offers us a profound insight: some of our own actions cause environmental degradation. Accepting and understanding this insight means that we are carefully reading the signs of the times.

In accepting our environmental responsibilities (this includes admitting our failings toward the earth and asking God for forgiveness), we find the opportunity and courage to proclaim God's merciful love to others. We become ideal evangelists for spreading the primary truth of Creation—that God cares deeply for us and all of Creation, including the natural world.

When we pray as individuals, we typically pray with the hope of coming closer to God. We long to enter more fully into life with Christ. We may turn away from God's call, or even resist it, at times. In the end, however, we are pulled by God's love to come closer, to walk with him again and to do his will.

Metanoia is a Greek word that means "a change of mind." It is used throughout the New Testament to suggest a turning *away* from sin and self-destruction. But it is also meant as a turning *toward* a new life, a fresh start, a choice and change that's much closer to what God has in mind for us. It's time for metanoia on behalf of the environment; a positive turning toward what God intends for creation will bring new life and new hope to our world.

Change, of course, is never easy. We have so many excuses at to why we shouldn't or can't change our lifestyles or our priorities. Living in a materialistic culture makes it hard to stand apart. Environmental activists

Did You Know?

About 6,800 gallons of water is needed to grow a day's worth of food for a family of four.

are urging us to "Reduce, Reuse, and Recycle," but the voices of consumerism urge us to "Buy, Use, Discard." However, as the prophet Micah says, we must do what "the Lord requires of you: only to do the right and to love goodness and to walk humbly with your God" (Mi 6:8).

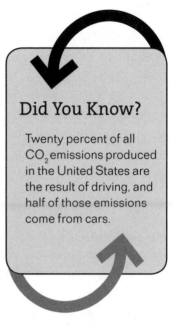

Did You Know?

Twenty percent of all CO_2 emissions produced in the United States are the result of driving, and half of those emissions come from cars.

Besides making personal changes to respond to the environmental crisis, we must evangelize others, urging them to change as well. We can get busy and spread the word about consuming less, recycling, respecting the needs of our planet, and answering the cry of the poor. All of this is a tremendous challenge. Nonetheless, this may be how God is calling you to tend his garden.

What changes—large and small—are you personally considering for the sake of environmental justice? Will you encourage others to do the same?

Promoting a sort of "Green gospel" will meet with resistance from some people you know. We live in a culture where individualism is a reigning paradigm. We hear much about the fear of personal commitments. Friendships are often only situational and marriages seem fragile. In our day, people are more reluctant to help strangers in need or distress.

As people of faith, we cannot be full of doom and gloom. We can't present ourselves as naysayers. Ideally, we should try to influence others with the timeless advice St. Francis of Assisi suggested for preaching the Gospel. "Preach the Gospel at all times; when necessary, use words." The power of example is the best persuasion. Seeing faithful marriages or watching strangers help those in need encourages all of us to make commitments and reach out. Ultimately, we cannot thrive or even survive as individuals, as communities, or as a culture without commitments. Renewing the face of the earth requires similar long-term commitment.

Take a look at that word *commitment*. Its prefix, *com-*, means "with" or "together," and can be found in the words *communion* and *community*. It makes perfect sense that the word commitment is related to those other words. The Church teaches that we are social by nature. Our faith lies in the central mystery of the Trinity—the relationship among Father, Son, and Holy Spirit. "Hence the whole Christian life is a communion with each of the divine persons" (*Catechism of the Catholic Church*, #259).

We long for communion with the Lord at the Eucharist. We also hunger to be in community with the Lord, the rest of the assembly, and with all of our brothers and sisters. Remaining independent and alone, without touching the lives of others, is a recipe for loneliness. Commitments are made for people and people for commitments.

How will the communities you belong to support your commitment to environmental justice?

While some human beings are in need of more because they already have so little, many others need to seriously examine their lifestyles to see how they should change for the sake of justice and respect for creation. How we live, rather than what we say, reveals our values. Do our values and lifestyle reflect the

Gospel? Or do they reflect the excesses, the "affluenza" of our culture?

Hopefully, we will teach our children to respect nature and adopt a sense of wonder and interest toward creation. Hopefully, our nation and other nations will address environmental problems, urging public officials to take their environmental responsibilities seriously. We will try to live in solidarity with the least among us. For the sake of future generations and for the planet itself, we will hear and answer God's call to conversion, committing ourselves to becoming responsible stewards of Creation.

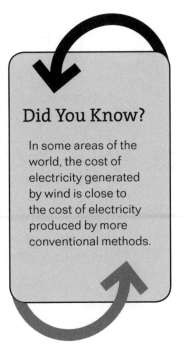

Did You Know?

In some areas of the world, the cost of electricity generated by wind is close to the cost of electricity produced by more conventional methods.

Hearing the Church

Now, read and reflect on what the Church has to say about commitment and hope, and their connection to conversion.

Benedict XVI is pope in a world that's increasingly frightened by environmental crisis and related poverty. But the Holy Father offers a reassuring voice, reminding us that Christians must be people of hope. The pope also reminds us that the God who created us will also sustain us.

> The liturgy itself teaches us this, when during the presentation of the gifts, the priest raises to God a prayer of blessing and petition over the bread and the wine, "fruit of the earth," "fruit of the vine" and "work of human hands." With these words, the rite not only includes in our offering

to God all human efforts and activity, but also leads us to see the world as God's creation, which brings forth everything we need for our sustenance. The world is not something indifferent, raw material to be utilized simply as we see fit. Rather, it is part of God's good plan, in which all of us are called to be sons and daughters in the one Son of God, Jesus Christ (cf. Ephesians 1:4–12). The justified concern about threats to the environment present in so many parts of the world is reinforced by Christian hope, which commits us to working responsibly for the protection of creation.

Sacramentum Caritatis (*The Sacrament of Charity*)
2007, #92

• • •

Monsignor Charles Murphy, a theologian from the diocese of Portland, Maine, is the former rector of the North American College in Rome and the author of several books on environmental theology.

Consumer choices and consumer demands are moral and cultural expressions of how we conceive of life. Is life all about working and spending and working more to have more to spend? Could not it rather be all about contemplation, what the pope (John Paul II) calls a "disinterested, unselfish and aesthetic attitude that is born of wonder in the presence of being and of beauty which enables one to see in visible things the message of the invisible God who created them? (*Centesimus Annus*, #37)."

The Good Life from a Catholic Perspective: The Challenge of Consumption,
in *Faithful Stewards of God's Creation: A Catholic Resource for Environmental Justice and Climate Change,*
Committee on Domestic and International Policy, United States Conference of Catholic Bishops, p. 28

• • •

Thomas Merton (1915–1968) was a Trappist monk of the Abbey of Gethsemani in Kentucky and one of the twentieth century's best-known authors of books on spirituality. Merton was also a poet, a social activist, and a student of comparative religions. Discussing community, he says,

> Community is not built by man, it is built by God. It is God's work and the basis of community is not just sociability but faith. This is what we need to see very clearly, because it is very important.
>
> . . . What really starts fighting is possessions. And people get into fights by preferring things to people. This is well developed in Christian theology, and therefore, for us, the importance of detachment from things, the importance of poverty, is that we are supposed to be free from things we might prefer to people. You can extend that to any limits you like—wherever things become more important than people we are in trouble. That is the crux of the whole matter.

Thomas Merton in Alaska: The Alaska Journals and Letters
New Directions Publishing Corp., 1989, p. 97

How do these reflections from Pope Benedict, Msgr. Murphy, and Thomas Merton make similar points about community and conversion?

Living the Message

What even one small community can accomplish is amazing. In the Detroit area, people pay attention to how St. Elizabeth Parish in Wyandotte is "living the message" of conversion.

When he talks about saving energy and other environmental issues, Fr. Charles Morris of St. Elizabeth Parish in Wyandotte, Michigan, likes to say, "We're *a part of* creation, not *apart from* it."

Wyandotte is a working-class inner-ring suburb of Detroit. The parish has only 230 Catholic households, or roughly five hundred Catholics. One reason it's still alive is that the parish has managed to stay in the black financially, in large part because of the 60 percent or so it saves in monthly gas and electric costs by a thoroughgoing program of energy efficiency.

Fr. Morris notes that St. Elizabeth's energy efficiency starts with solar electrical panels, a wind turbine, and a solar water heating system on the rectory roof. It has switched from incandescent lighting fixtures to fluorescent or compact fluorescent lamps for all the rectory and church lighting. It now uses LEDs (light emitting diodes) for illuminated exit signs, and has added a new energy-efficient boiler and reduced-pressure water systems to cut water usage.

The list of energy saving measures that Fr. Morris cites goes on: they use block glass in the church basement, installing new windows with an R-9 insulation rating. They have installed 24/7 programmable thermostats to minimize heating or cooling during hours that buildings are not in use.

In the first five years of moving toward greater energy efficiency, from 1997 to 2002, "we reduced our peak energy demand 60 percent" in the church and school, he says. As a result, the electric company reduced the parish's peak demand charge by $300 a month.

Fr. Morris says that the parish regularly tracks its energy use by computer: "We found in the 11 months from April 2007 to March 2008 we reduced our gas [usage] by 11 percent. That was 29,000 pounds of CO_2 kept out of the atmosphere." He adds that even though the winter of 2007–08 was a cold one and the price of gas had increased, "we actually spent $300 less on utilities."

Fr. Morris says that even though it will take years to recoup the costs of their energy-saving investments it's worth doing it from a faith perspective. "It's sacramental. It's witness," he says. "Human beings were put in the Garden of Eden to tend it, not to cover it with asphalt. How do we relate to God's creation in terms of glorifying it, and not trashing it for future generations? This is really a huge, ultimate life issue."

For Fr. Morris, glorifying God's creation means a smart and frugal use of resources. How would you make the same case—that small, practical, cost-saving measures can make a difference?

What Can We Do?

As you continue to reflect on these voices from our Church, consider and discuss the following Action Options. Some of these projects might help you and your group develop new approaches to conversion and commitment. Some are projects you will pursue personally. Others are more effective when done with your group.

Action Options

- Help organize a parish or neighborhood Green Committee to help build understanding and acceptance of environmental risks and challenges.

- Find out more about the three Rs of environmentalism: Reduce, Reuse, Recycle. Take a week or two to consider your home and lifestyle. Then make at least one small change in each of the three categories.

- Call your local government about disposal locations for hazardous wastes like car batteries, paints, appliances, etc.

- Sponsor a day of prayer for environmental justice in your community.

- Investigate energy-efficient lighting and heating/cooling options for your own home.

- Recycle your paper, glass, plastics, and other waste. Call your local government or waste collection service to find out if they offer a recycling plan.

- Write a "letter to the editor" for your newspaper to promote environmental justice, pointing out how simple "green" practices can help.

- Use rechargeable batteries.

- Stop or cut down on the use of disposable products like paper plates, napkins, and plastic utensils and cups.

- Ask local groceries to stock organic items or eco-labeled goods not currently available from your local shops.

- Buy locally grown produce.

- Buy organic fruits, vegetables, cotton clothing, and hemp-fiber products.

- Use tap water instead of bottled water. If you must buy bottled water, buy from a local source that uses recyclable plastic or glass.

- Reduce the temperature on your water heater.

- Wrap insulating blankets around water heater and water pipes to keep the heat from escaping.

Write down your choices here:

Individual Action Commitment

Group Action Commitment:

Closing Prayer

→

Opening

Reflect quietly together while a song is played that celebrates renewal and commitment to justice. You might consider "Shepherd Me, O God" or "Gather Us In," both by Marty Haugen.

Scripture Reading

Read together Mark 10:17–27, the Gospel story about the rich young man. Now share ideas about what this reading could mean for people today. Does Jesus really expect everyone to "sell what you have and give it to the poor"? Does this story have a message for everyone?

Petitions

Offer petitions for the strength and courage to make commitments to change on behalf of environmental justice and our brothers and sisters. Offer prayers for a renewed world. Use a petition response such as "O God, Renew the face of the world."

Prayer Pledge

As a group, read together the following pledge of commitment for the environment. Or, divide the group in two so that each half of the group can alternate in reading the prayer pledge stanzas.

> *Pledge of Commitment to Protect and Heal God's Creation*
>
> We have come to renew our covenant with God
> and with one another in Christ Jesus, our Lord.
> We have come to help protect God's creation.

We have come as followers of Jesus to commit ourselves anew to one another and to heal injustice and poverty.

We have come to stand together against all threats to life.

We have come to discover some new beauty in God's creation every day: the sunrise and sunset; birds, flowers, and trees; rainbows in the sky; the stars; and the many forms of life in the forest.

We have come to listen to the "music of the universe"—water flowing over rocks, the wind, trees bending in the wind, raindrops pattering on the roof.

We will remember always that God speaks to us through the beauty of his creation, and we will try our best to answer God's call to reverence all that He has created.

Faithful Stewards of God's Creation: A Catholic Resource for Environmental Justice and Climate Change
Committees on Domestic and International Policy,
United States Conference of Catholic Bishops, 2001, p. 48

RESOURCES

Books

Christensen, Drew, S.J. and Walter Grazer. *And God Saw That It Was Good: Catholic Theology and the Environment.* United States Conference of Catholic Bishops, 1996.

Compendium of the Social Doctrine of the Church. Pontifical Council for Justice and Peace, Libreria Editrice Vatican City, 2004. Available through the United States Conference of Catholic Bishops.

Edwards, Dennis. *Ecology at the Heart of Faith.* Orbis Books, Maryknoll, New York, 2006

Fragomeni, Richard and John Pawlikowski. *The Ecological Challenge: Ethical, Liturgical, and Spiritual Responses.* Liturgical Press, Collegeville Minnesota, 1994.

Global Climate Change: A Plea for Dialogue, Prudence and the Common Good. United States Conference of Catholic Bishops, June 2001.

God's Creation Cries for Justice, Climate Change: Impact and Response. Participant Packet 2008–09. Just Faith Ministries and Catholic Coalition on Climate Change, Louisville, Kentucky, 2007.

The Green Bible. Harper One, Harper Collins Publishers, 2008.

Hill, Bernard. *Christian Faith and the Environment: Making Vital Connections.* Orbis Books, 1998.

Irwin, Kevin and Edmund Pellegrino. *Preserving the Creation: Environmental Theology and Ethics.* Georgetown University Press, 1994.

Keenan, Sr. Majorie. *Care for Creation: Human Activity and the Environment.* Libreria Editrice Vatican City, 2000.

———. *From Stockholm to Johannesburg: An Historical Overview of the Concern of the Holy See for the Environment—1972–2002.* Vatican City, 2002.

Murphy, Charles. *At Home on the Earth: Foundations for a Catholic Ethic of the Environment.* Crossroads, 1989.

Renewing the Earth: An Invitation to Reflection and Action on Environment in Light of Catholic Social Teaching. United States Conference of Catholic Bishops, November 14, 1991.

Silecchia, Lucia. "*Discerning the Environmental Perspective of Pope Benedict XVI.*" Journal of Catholic Social Thought, Vol. 4, No. 2, Summer 2007, pp. 227–269.

Websites

Catholic Coalition on Climate Change (CCCC)

The CCCC, in cooperation with other national Catholic partners, seeks to contribute a distinctive and authentic Catholic voice to the public debate about the environment, providing educational and organizing resources to dioceses, parishes, and other Catholic organizations.

www.catholicsandclimatechange.org

Catholic Conservation Center

The mission of the Catholic Conservation Center is to promote ecology, environmental justice, and the stewardship of creation in light of sacred scripture and the living tradition of the Roman Catholic Church.

www.conservation.catholic.org

Department of Justice, Peace, and Human Development

The Department of Justice, Peace, and Human Development (formerly Social Development and World Peace) of the United States Conference of Catholic Bishops assists the bishops of the United States in their work to address domestic and international policy. The department provides information on Catholic social teaching and on the Church's positions on issues of justice and peace. Resources are available for diocesan social action leaders, parish social ministry leaders, priests and deacons, Catholic educators, and others.

www.usccb.org/sdwp/ejp

National Religious Partnership for the Environment

The National Religious Partnership for the Environment is an interfaith coalition of major religious communities dedicated to caring for God's creation. Its members include the Coalition on the Environment and Jewish Life; the Evangelical Environmental Network; the National Council of Churches, USA; and the United States Conference of Catholic Bishops.

www.nrpe.org

The Vatican

The Vatican's website provide a wealth of information and documentation of speeches and official statements of the pope and the Vatican.

www.Vatican.va

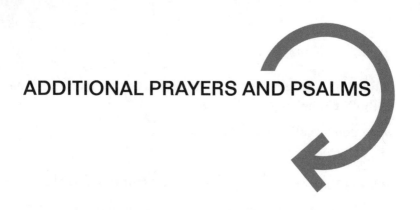

ADDITIONAL PRAYERS AND PSALMS

In group settings you may want to invite a different person to read each verse of the prayer or Psalm.

The Canticle of the Sun

Most High, all powerful, good Lord,
Yours are the praises, the glory, the honor, and all blessing.
To you alone, Most High, do they belong,
and no one is worthy to mention your name.

Be praised, my Lord, through all your creatures,
especially through my lord Brother Sun, who brings the day;
he is beautiful and radiant in all his splendor!
Of you, Most High, he bears the likeness.

Praise be you, my Lord, through Sister Moon and the stars,
in heaven you formed them clear and precious and beautiful.

Praised be you, my Lord, through Brother Wind,
and through the air, cloudy and serene,
and every kind of weather
through which you give sustenance to your creatures.

Praised be you, my Lord, through Sister Water,
which is very useful and humble and precious and chaste.

Praised be you, my Lord, through Brother Fire,
through whom you light the night
and he is beautiful and playful and robust and strong.

Praised be you, my Lord, through Sister Mother Earth,
who sustains us and governs us
and who produces varied fruits with colored flowers and herbs.

Praised be you, my Lord, through those who give pardon for
   your love,
and bear infirmity and tribulation.
Blessed are those who endure in peace
for by you, Most High, they shall be crowned.

Amen.

—From the hymn by St. Francis of Assisi

St. Patrick's Breastplate

I bind unto myself today
The strong name of the Trinity,
By invocation of the same
The Three in One and One in Three.
I bind this today to me forever.

I bind unto myself today
The virtues of the star lit heaven,
The glorious sun's life giving ray,
The whiteness of the moon at even,
The flashing of the lightning free,
The whirling wind's tempestuous shocks,
The stable earth, the deep salt sea
Around the old eternal rocks.

I bind unto myself today
The power of God to hold and lead,
His eye to watch, His might to stay,
His ear to hearken to my need.
The wisdom of my God to teach,
His hand to guide, His shield to ward;
The word of God to give me speech,
His heavenly host to be my guard.

Christ be with me, Christ within me,
Christ behind me, Christ before me,
Christ beside me, Christ to win me,
Christ to comfort and restore me.
Christ beneath me, Christ above me,
Christ in quiet, Christ in danger,
Christ in hearts of all that love me,
Christ in mouth of friend and stranger.

I bind unto myself the name,
The strong name of the Trinity,
By invocation of the same,
The Three in One and One in Three.
By whom all nature hath creation,
Eternal Father, Spirit, Word:
Praise to the Lord of my salvation,
Salvation is of Christ the Lord.

—Adapted from the translation by Cecil Alexander, 1889
The original Gaelic poem by St. Patrick was
likely written in the early fifth century

O God, our Father, you have set us over all the works of your hands. You have shared with us your creative power to build a world of peace and justice—a world in which everyone can live as brothers and sisters endowed with human dignity as members of your human family.

Grant us the grace to believe firmly that you have given us sufficient resources for this purpose. Show us how to use them generously to provide food, decent shelter, education, and meaningful employment for all in your family.

Gracious God, strengthen us with humility and wisdom. Teach us to be thankful for the precious mystery of life that you have made ours. Bless our efforts to promote the total development of each and every human being that all might reach the fullness of their potential and dignity as your sons and daughters.

Amen.

—Adapted from a prayer by Terence Cardinal Cooke
Archbishop of New York, 1968–1983

From Psalm 72

All: Justice shall flourish in his time, and fullness of peace
forever.

Justice shall flower in his days,
and profound peace, till the moon be no more.
May he rule from sea to sea,
and from the River to the ends of the earth.

All: Justice shall flourish in his time, and fullness of peace
forever.

For he shall rescue the poor when they cry out,
and the afflicted when they have no one to help.
He shall have pity for the lowly and the poor,
the lives of the poor he shall save.

All: Justice shall flourish in his time, and fullness of peace
forever.

May his name be blessed forever;
as long as the sun his name shall remain.
In him shall all the tribes of the earth be blessed;
all nations shall proclaim his happiness!

All: Justice shall flourish in his time, and fullness of peace
forever.

From Psalm 85

All: O God, let us see your kindness, and grant us your
      salvation.

      I will hear what God Proclaims;
      for he proclaims peace to his people.
      Near indeed is his salvation to those who fear him,
      glory dwelling in our land.

All: O God, let us see your kindness, and grant us your
      salvation.

      Kindness and truth shall meet
      justice and peace shall kiss.
      Truth shall spring out of the earth,
      and justice shall look down from heaven.

All: O God, let us see your kindness, and grant us your
      salvation.

      The Lord himself will give his benefits;
      our land shall yield its increase.
      Justice shall walk before him,
      and prepare the way of his steps.

All: O God, let us see your kindness, and grant us your
      salvation.

Walter E. Grazer served as the Director of the Environmental Justice Program for the United States Conference of Catholic Bishops from 1993 to 2007. He is currently a consultant for the National Religious Partnership for the Environment, an inter-religious coalition that includes the United States Conference of Catholic Bishops. He holds an M.A. in international relations, a Masters of social work, and a B.A. in philosophy. Grazer is co-editor of *And God Saw That It Was Good: Catholic Theology and the Environment.*

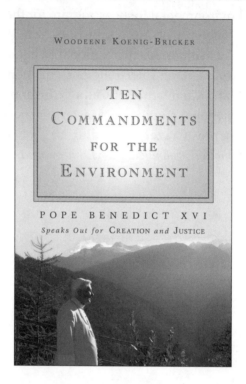